Times
to
Treasure

Presented to: _____

From: _____

On the Occasion of: _____

_____

Times to Treasure

Alma Barkman

Moody Press
Chicago

Times to Treasure

All scripture quotations, except those noted otherwise, are from the *New American Standard Bible*, © 1960, 1962, 1963, 1968, 1971, 1972, 1973, and 1975 by The Lockman Foundation, and are used by permission.

ISBN: 0-8024-2072-9

Printed in the United States of America

Design and Photographs: Koechel/Peterson Design, Minneapolis, MN

Acknowledgments:

The following first appeared in the Steinbach, Manitoba, *Carillon* and are reprinted by permission: "To the Man in My Life"; "Diamonds in the Dough"; "The Present"; "Tribute to a Rural Mother"; "Is the End in Sight?" (titled "The Solitaire" in this volume); "Gathering Eggs with Uncle Jim"; "City Kids and Country Cows"; "The Winner!"; "A Visit to Grandpa's; and "A Path for All Seasons."

The poem "Day One" is from *Home Life*, Sept. 1974. © Copyright 1974 The Sunday School Board of the Southern Baptist Convention. All rights reserved. Used by permission.

"Hospitals Make Me Sick" and "I Wonder Where the Yellow Went" ("Old Ivory" in this volume) are reprinted by permission of the Winnipeg Free Press.

"Our Life Is a Floral Arrangement" ("God's Bouquet" in this volume); "There Is Nearby a Sheltered Cove" ("Harbor of Prayer" in this volume); and "In the Valley of the Shadows" were first published by Cathedral Press, Inc., and are reprinted by permission.

To
Lyle, Brent, Gae, and Glen,
the four "jewels" in the Barkman family setting.

Contents

Times to Treasure

Buried Treasure

*And He said to them,
'Therefore every scribe who
has become a disciple of the
kingdom of heaven is like
a head of a household,
who brings forth out of his
treasure things new and old.'*
(Matthew 13:52).

Sometimes I wonder about You, Lord.
My tongue is the pen of a ready writer,
and yet You want me to talk
about the same old things.
What can I say
about children with dirty faces
and gum in their hair,
or a teenager overhauling his jalopy
in the driveway,
or the tomcat uprooting my petunias,
except to tell the truth?
And whoever heard of a scribe
wearing curlers and apron?
You say this mess is my *treasury*?
My storehouse of ideas?
I'm sorry, Lord,
but You and I aren't seeing things
from the same perspective.
You say if I stand over here
near You...
You're right!
Just hold Your Light up a little
and give me a chance to reflect.
Those treasures have got to be right here,
somewhere.

1
Love Letters

To the Man in My Life:

To the most excellent governor...greetings (Acts 23:26).

Back in the days of our courtship, I decided to pave the way to your heart with a homemade pie. I felt sure I could conquer you with one piece. I did, too, in a way. The blueberry filling turned out to be a combination of purple rubber and stiff tapioca. It stretched but it had no bounce. The crust? If I had only made the pie larger you would have had sufficient leather for both moccasins.

You married me anyway, sort of forgiving but not forgetting. When the buns would have made better cannon fodder, they were, in your opinion, pretty good compared to the blueberry pie. With minor variations, it has been the same theme for twenty years. I am a good cook, relatively speaking.

If your stomach stands up for another five years, we shall celebrate our silver anniversary. By then I suppose we may be grandparents, and our sons will find it hard to believe that dear old Dad actually anticipated the challenge of the maternity ward four times in ten years. Each time, you beamed with delight as lusty cries issued anew the proclamation of fatherhood.

I remember your watching our firstborn— a son who arrived two months prematurely. He was a tiny scrap of humanity I thought only a mother could love. But there you stood, gazing into the incubator with admiration equal to mine. Others may have thought all those trips to the nursery to "see" if he had gained an ounce were unwarranted. You never complained, just smiled at my maternal longings, as new and strange to me as they were to you.

Showers of blessing are found in the climate of parenthood. There are times, of course, when children have a way of dampening either your lap or your spirit, or both. Ours are no exception. You learned sooner than I did to "let a smile be your umbrella."

When I grow discouraged with the "line upon line, precept upon precept" method of training children, and spare no words in saying so, you often retort, "Yes, but..." You believe in giving people the benefit of the doubt. I half suspect there are times when you apply the same theory to me.

You are convinced that the best therapy for discouragement is the discipline of hard

work. I remember becoming an outspoken victim of social pressure. Why could we not have things others took for granted? A home of our own? Nice furniture? Family vacations? Strangely enough, keeping the old nose to the grindstone blurred the visions of greener pastures. The next time I was tempted to peek over the fence, I could see things in better perspective. You have shown me that achievement produces its own unique brand of contentment.

As a result, I realize now that the house we own is not nearly as valuable to me as the experience of building it together. And now that I could probably afford ready-made clothes, I find a bigger satisfaction in sewing my own. Nice furniture? That lost its appeal over the years, too, partly because the children were so attached to the old relics we had collected that they hated to part with them. When at long last we put our foot down and bought a new chesterfield, the boys dragged the old one down to the "wreck" room. The arms are all tattered, and the stuffing sticks out of random holes, but it is a reminder from whence we came. Every so often we collapse into it and count our blessings.

It has always been a source of encouragement to me that, if it is within your power, hardships only come to "pass"; they seldom come to stay. Nothing seems to challenge you more than the impossible. You are not foolhardy. You just take issue with some of the current trends that say a man must fit within a certain mold in order to succeed. You proved to me, and others, that a man who is willing to sacrifice and ready to work has a head start. Your independent nature prescribes that the best place to find a helping hand is at the end of your own arm, although now and then you are glad of a little support—mine, to be exact.

Despite the fact that you have been a hard worker all these years, you still find time for the finer things of life. You are not a great musician, as great musicians go. But after a long day at the office and an evening of carpentry, you will sit down at the piano, with a red hanky dangling from your hind pocket and a pencil still stuck behind one ear, and rattle off something like "Put on Your Old Gray Bonnet." The kids look at me with gleeful suppressed grins. Guess Dad is not such a bad old square after all!

Then we have a little concert all our own, with the toddlers banging wooden spoons on the dishpan and the teenagers improvising on trumpet and clarinet. As in your daily life, the sacred and the secular both find expression, and often the notes of "Bless This House" echo to the rafters and bounce out into the darkness on the heels of "Old Black Joe."

And then, suddenly, as if to summon sleep, you play "Abide with Me." The boys pack away their instruments, the toddlers yawn as they shuffle off to bed. A hush descends upon the house—angels passing by, no doubt, or maybe hovering.

You so seldom get a moment's peace and quiet that I hate to break the silence, but just this once I'll take the liberty to whisper, "Thank you."

Dear Son

You are our letter, written in our hearts, known and read by all men; being manifested that you are a letter of Christ, cared for by us, written not with ink, but with the Spirit of the living God, not on tablets of stone, but on tablets of human hearts (2 Corinthians 3:2-3).

Dear Son,

So you're off to Bible college! A week ago you manfully undertook the job of cleaning out your room. Now eighteen years of living is not thrown out in one rash moment (at least I hope not!), and so you took your time sorting through the accumulation—disposing of this, keeping that, delaying some decisions until later.

And so you should. Spontaneity has its place, but not when you are about to embark on an important move. At the same time, we both chuckled at the amount of trash you toted out to the garbage. What you wanted to keep seemed small by comparison. That's life, son. You may do a lot of living that may not mean much later on. Or maybe three years of study will be condensed into a certificate, nine by twelve. But don't be fooled by people who would equate quality only with things tangible. If that were true, the crown would not be much compared to the cross, and we have reason to believe otherwise.

For the moment, however, we live in a world that requires a very practical approach. And so you backed the car up to the doorway and in went the necessities for college living.

There was the lumpy pillow and the homemade quilt and the temperamental alarm clock, the box of mechanic's tools you keep under your bed, and the favorite records you hope to enjoy. There was the suitcase you never really appreciated until now, and an assortment of clothes you had rounded up at the last minute, all of which needed alterations, or so it seemed.

The next morning you seemed rather reluctant to leave, and I thought I saw a faint resemblance to the little boy who had started school exactly thirteen years ago today. He had hovered about on the doorstep in much the same way, or do you remember?

At last, however, you took a deep breath, squared your shoulders and left, with the sound of your old jalopy shattering the morning air.

We joined you at the campus a few days later to see for ourselves what Bible college was all about. I could sense you had some reservations about adjusting, but your outlook on the whole was optimistic. I was glad of that. Only the foolhardy plunge in with complete abandon. The wise man feels his way along. "Trust and Obey," the words of the hymn, were reminding us as we gathered for a chapel service. Wise advice for a young person away from home for the first time, but not so easy for his mother.

I know now a little of Hannah's struggle to leave her firstborn at the house of the Lord. In fact the song was conveying her motives very well: *We never can prove the delights of His love until all on the altar we lay.* As for me, I was having trouble sorting out my sacrifice: Was it the gifted young man with the bass voice beside me, or the four-pound premature baby I had brought home from the hospital eighteen years before? Somehow they did not seem like one and the same person.

Meanwhile you sat stiffly between your father and me, and all three of us were painfully aware that this moment marked that point of separation which we had known one day would come. True, we had worked toward it, planned for it, and hoped for it, but somehow we never expected it would come so soon. Within an hour we would be leaving you on your own, and the idea was just a little disturbing.

At that point, a very perceptive organist began to play "Be Still My Soul," and a sense of peace swept over me as I realized anew that the Lord *is* on thy side. I think you sensed it too, for I could feel your broad young shoulders slowly relax as you took to heart the words of that favorite old hymn, which you yourself have often played in times of stress and turmoil.

As we drove away from the campus that night, I felt I was reliving a scene from the past. Eighteen years before I had given birth to a tiny boy, and the pediatrician had said, "I'm sorry, but you'll have to go home without him. We plan to keep him here in the incubator for a few weeks longer."

In my heart I knew it was for your good, but I shall never forget the pain of walking down the steps of that hospital without you, knowing that I had to entrust our firstborn to the care of strangers.

And here I was again, experiencing almost the same feelings for the second time, except that both of us had matured considerably in the intervening years.

If I am convinced of your "calling" (and I am), then I must believe everything will work out fine, and it will, although not necessarily the way I might expect it should. I suppose I would have to say that my soul is in relatively good shape. It's just my tear ducts that are giving me problems.

Love,
Mom, alias Hannah

P.S. You forgot your "little cloak." Shall I bring it when I come?

Dear Daughter

What we are in word by letters when absent, such persons we are also in deed when present (2 Corinthians 10:11).

Dear Daughter,

The wedding bells are pealing in the distance, and you, dear girl, are still out shopping for an apartment.

I know just what you have in mind. A cozy little place, convenient to work, just big enough for two. You want a breakfast nook that will match your set of dishes, a living room with space for a stereo, and a bedroom that will do justice to the crocheted spread your grandmother has tucked away for you as a wedding gift. The apartment should be near a supermarket because you can't really afford two cars, and a patio would be just super, and gold colored rugs —why, you couldn't ask for more!

But alas! You can't find what you want. I can just imagine the frustration in your eyes when you come home night after night and the only "decent" place you have found is twice too expensive. Absolutely bewildered, you ask yourself over and over, "Where are we going to *live?*" And you twist your engagement ring around and around your finger as you pray, "Lord, please help us to find an apartment, *soon.*"

Let me give you some advice, if I may. I know a little of what it's like to dream, to picture yourself established in your very first apartment, to imagine what it will be like to cook and clean, and take care of that very special fellow who has chosen you to be his bride. The supper will *always* be on time, the floors will *all* be spotless, and absolutely everything will be just perfect.

But that is just in dreams, my girl. And dreams are not sufficient to make miracles come true. So don't be disillusioned if that very first apartment falls short of what you have in mind. Oh, you'll shed a few tears as I once did when your father and I set up housekeeping on the third floor of a creaking old house with nothing much more than orange crates for cupboards. The string that held the plastic curtain across a shelf of hand-me-down dishes used to get slack once in a while, and my spirits drooped accordingly.

And the big old iron bedstead must have belonged to Henry VIII. It sagged in the middle, and we always rolled to the center of the bed, even when we'd just had a fight.

Now I ask you, What do you do in a case like that, except make up?

My dreams of hanging out a sparkling wash in a yard surrounded by lilac bushes quickly dissipated in a dingy basement as I tried to operate a cantankerous wringer washer while a shrewd landlord breathed down my neck for "feefty cenz, pleez." Then it was up three flights of rickety stairs to hang my wash from a balcony that reeked of garlic, dill, and onions.

Suffering as I was from morning sickness, such strong aromas were not exactly conducive to health. I know. I know. You think that nowadays these things don't happen, that the stork is a rather sedate old creature who courteously waits for an official invitation before taking up residence on your chimney. Don't you believe a word of it! He's a wily old bird just itching to dispense his special brand of baby propaganda, *especially* when he sees a brand new nest just brimming over with love.

I suppose what I'm really trying to say is that dreams must be focused in reality or else marriage becomes a nightmare of unfulfilled wishes. It is so easy to be carried away by the *things* we'd like to have, when in fact they are not at all essential to a happy marriage.

Even though I detested those old orange crate cupboards, they served their purpose every bit as well as the stained mahogany type we now have. And that sagging bed—well, I can't be too grateful for the many times it encouraged us to settle our disputes the right way—locked in one another's embrace, tears of genuine forgiveness trickling onto the same pillow.

Looking back, I am even thankful for that landlord, whose rigid demands simply served as a prod toward furthering our independence in a home of our own. His "feefty cenz, pleez" became a standing joke, a term we use yet for any favor we deem ridiculous.

And how shall I classify a pregnancy that was at one and the same time so awkwardly inconvenient and yet so richly rewarding? Let me put it this way: If I could know with certainty that we had done our part to equip you for maturity, I believe I would even be so bold as to drop a hint in the old stork's ear concerning the early delivery of a bundle labeled Fragile: Handle with Care. There is nothing in this world that will test your capabilities as a wife and mother like the arrival of your first child.

But what has all of this to do with apartment hunting? Simply this: Don't dismiss everything within reach as being unsuitable, for if there is one asset within marriage that will prove to be invaluable, it's the willingness to adapt to existing conditions. Not the way things might have been or should have been, or even how they will be, but how they are today, this moment. That is what we must learn to accept. "Not My will, but Thine be done." Remember?

Love,
Mom

2
Family Album

Growing with God

My fruit is better than gold, even pure gold,
And my yield than choicest silver (Proverbs 8:19).

Last fall that botanical nightmare in my backyard finally yielded up its secrets for another year, but not very willingly, mind you. To shorten an interminably long story, it was just a simple case of my standing on the porch, wagging a purple thumb in the general direction of the back garden, and threatening something horrible like, "You grow or *else!*" Ominous as this may sound to successful gardeners, it actually works, in an indirect sort of way. By indirect I mean that before things got to this point, I tried every conceivable method known to horticulture to provide fresh vegetables for the family.

Contrary to general opinion, I can't blame it on the soil. Being rather citified (by circumstance, not choice) I invested in a bag of "nutrient fertilizer" that was supposed to enrich the garden plot. Instead it just depleted my pocketbook. It was no fool who coined the expression "farmer's gold"—it was a suburban gardener like me. If some enterprising farmer would like to get rich overnight, he should just put a For Sale sign on that mound of nuggets out behind his barn. The result would be another Klondike. Were I to spread the original product generously over the backyard, however, the neighbors, all armed with barbeque forks, would descend upon me in droves. So aside from the fact that I refuse to declare bankruptcy in favor of quality, neither do I expect to risk physical extermination in favor of quantity. I wistfully resort to more refined fertilizers, with dignified names, delicate scent, and dubious value per pound.

To complicate matters, the seeds in my garden have a loathsome habit of getting out of line. I am certain they roll around underground, devising evil schemes to aggravate me. When at long last the rows appear, it looks like they were planted by the neighborhood merrymaker the morning after the night before. Nevertheless I am the one with the sore head, and the pain reaches right down to that rusty hinge in the small of my back.

Anyway, the garden is up and that's the main thing. Or is it? Now comes an infinite number of bugs, worms, beetles, grasshoppers, cabbage moths, and you-name-its. Armed with an even greater number of chemical cures and kill-it-alls, I begin the onslaught. It's just nip and tuck between me and the worms as to who gets the first radish. Those worms have an uncanny sense of timing. I finally get it all down pat as to what kills whom and who kills what, but by then the bugs have left for greener gardens.

After standing over that garden patch day and night coaxing it along, I begin to feel my back will be permanently bent into the shape of a hairpin. Finally I get down on my knees and implore things to grow. About this point I realize I'm not just growing a garden. I'm cultivating personalities.

Take the lettuce, for instance. It sits there sulking until in desperation I go and buy some at the corner store. In about two days I have so much lettuce in my garden I'm giving it away to every available friend and enemy in a vain attempt to keep it from forming a hedge.

And the carrots! Other folks grow tall handsome carrots with broad shoulders and slender waistlines. Not me. Mine even refuse to surrender themselves from the ground, and no wonder! With figures like they have, I'd be ashamed of myself too. Last year there were some real characters in the underworld—fat ladies in toreador pants, mermaids, corkscrews, and Siamese twins with dimpled knees. One carrot displayed genuine apologetic appeal, much like a little boy standing in line at the bathroom when he can't wait much longer.

If I didn't feel so responsible! The very sight of anything green and growing is my call to arms. My five-foot frame dwarfed by an unwieldy selection of garden tools, I stagger toward the house at close of day with images of ragweeds drooping before my sun-dazzled eyes. What's this I see? The neighbor has left a gorgeous basket of fresh vegetables on the back step, and here I am slaving away from morning till night with not one edible result. (Yet!)

It was just such a discouraging comparison as this, however, that compelled me to make up my mind. Next year I'll forgo planting a single seed. Gone will be the tang of fertilizer first thing in spring. Gone will be the creaking back, blistered hands, sun-scorched arms, and peeling nose. Gone will be the cans, bottles, and bags of insecticides and weed killers lining the garage walls. Gone will be the collection of hoes, rakes, spades, and forks propped up against the back porch. Like so many other endeavors, it's just not worth the trouble.

I stubbornly ignore the seed catalog lying there on my desk in all its glory. Instead, very self-righteously, I open the Bible beside it.

What's this I read? "So then neither the one who plants nor the one who waters is anything, but God who causes the growth."*

I wilt under this gentle reproof, determined to let God have His way, even when it comes to *my* garden. "For we are God's fellow-workers..."†

Better make that our garden.

I reach for the phone. "Hello? Green Thumb Seed Company? I'm going into business with Someone Else next year, and we'll need an extra large order of seeds. When can they be delivered? Fine! We want to get an early start. What kind of partnership? Oh, He has the know-how and I expect to do the work. What name will we go by? Oh, now, let me see...what about Eden Enterprises? Yes, that's it! No, better make that Eden Enterprises, *Unlimited*. There's nothing the two of us can't do together."

*1 Corinthians 3:7.
†1 Corinthians 3:9a

Diamonds in the Dough

Like an earring of gold and an ornament of fine gold
Is a wise reprover to a listening ear (Proverbs 25:12).

Regardless of how much you pay for it at the supermarket, you still keep telling yourself you can't bake bread. Nonsense! Why even your most humble endeavor would be a vast improvement over those wheat husks and sesame seeds they glue together down at the bakery. (Or have you never wondered if that's what becomes of surplus wallpaper paste?)

Be honest now. Don't you always feel a little insecure when that hubby of yours is distracted by one of those wholesome gals who serve him homemade bread? You squirm as he raves on and on about it, and somehow you feel so utterly helpless. But not anymore! Now you can compete on an equal basis. The day you take those first golden loaves of homemade bread from the oven, hubby will literally be eating out of your hand.

Not only that, but once you perfect the product, baking your own bread will give you a distinct advantage over those annoying but less enterprising individuals known as neighbors. Remember how you shudder every time that model housekeeper across the street comes pussyfooting up your cluttered driveway? Or how you flinch when the fashion plate next door catches you in last year's dress? Well, never mind. Just dust the flour from your apron, put your feet up, and bask in a glory all your own. Can't you anticipate that smug feeling you will enjoy as the aroma of homemade bread permeates every corner of your kitchen and escapes out the open window? Eat your heart out, neighbors!

There is even something about baking bread that seems to bring out the maternal instincts. Perhaps it is because we have this concept of an old-fashioned wife and mother bent over the kitchen table, punching dough. The kettle whistles softly in the background, and the children scamper about on the oval braided rug.

A few hours later, we see all the young ones eagerly reaching out for fresh slices of homemade bread, spread thickly with butter and jam.

Frankly, I won't even guess just how close you

may come to fulfilling that perfect image. Maybe all you need to complete the picture is the homemade bread. So what if your first attempt doesn't win first prize at the county fair? It will be every bit as filling, if not more so. Why even the teenager's appetite may grind to a halt after two or three slabs. Don't be alarmed, however, as he'll pull through. Just keep telling yourself that practice makes perfect. Given enough time, bread—like mankind—rises to fullest heights even under the most trying conditions.

What about long-range prospects? Unless you bake bread on a regular basis, you may never realize the hidden benefits that lie buried just beneath the surface.

Did you know, for instance, that a marriage is supposed to be happier if the wife bakes her own bread? The underlying theory is that whenever conflicts arise, she transfers her frustrations to the ball of dough. Depending upon her mood, she may punch it, wring its neck, or flatten it out—in short, she just inflicts whatever damage is necessary to

relieve her pent-up emotions. The more angry she is, the better the dough. In fact, it just bounces back for more, which isn't true of husbands in general.

There is also this matter of bread being the staff of life. Nutritionally speaking, there is no end to the things you can sneak into homemade bread. Leftover cereals, stale milk, bacon drippings, the water drained from vegetables—I use them all. What the kids don't know certainly hasn't hurt them. Sometimes I wonder if it's because the bread is so nourishing or whether they have developed an immunity to less adulterated products. They say you can build up a resistance to anything.

I once entered a loaf of brown bread in competition at the local fair. The judge seemed to think it merited first prize. Stumped for a more suitable comment, the home economist told me it had a very unique flavor. She paled considerably when I listed the contents. Some people have weak stomachs.

Last but not least is the economic factor to be considered. Will you really save money baking your own bread? I suppose it depends on how successful you are. Let's put it this way though. For the price you pay at the corner store, you could feed every second batch to the dog and still come out on top.

If you really mean business, go out and drag home a hundred-pound bag of flour. Once the budget has recovered from the initial shock, you'll discover one of two things: (1) a marked *decrease* in the grocery bill or (2) a marked *increase* in the size of your dog.

In the final analysis, whether or not you find it rewarding to bake your own bread depends upon your sense of values. You may insist there are more rewarding experiences in life than merely stretching your food dollar. And with flour the price of gold dust, baking bread may sound like a risky prospect only the foolhardy would attempt. On the other hand, if you enjoy a certain spirit of adventure, why not rise to the challenge?

They used to claim there was "gold in them thar hills." I preferred to stake my bottom dollar on something edible, like homemade bread. With a few years' experience under my belt, I am more convinced than ever that "there's diamonds in this here dough." Why, I can even see them sparkle in a young fellow's eyes when he charges home from football practice and fills up the hollows in his uniform with fresh slices of homemade bread, spread thickly with butter and jam.

Old Ivory

Who can open the doors of his face?
Around his teeth there is terror (Job 41:14).

I overheard a woman on the bus say she rather enjoyed going to the dentist. People like that shouldn't be allowed at large.

Who in his right senses finds any pleasure in a trip to the dentist? Besides, it's costly. I have to hire somebody to push me up the steps. By the time we reach the top, my legs have buckled under me and I have to crawl through the door on my hands and knees.

Then it happens. You'd think a person in my position would be granted the privilege of remaining anonymous. But, no! The receptionist takes one look and in a voice designed to penetrate outer space, announces shrilly, "Mrs. Barkman has arrived."

The waiting room is jammed to capacity with yowling kids, fidgety mothers, and crotchety old men whose lower plates are irritating them. For a moment there is dead silence. I pick myself up, stagger toward a lime green chair, and collapse into it. The noise resumes and slowly gains momentum. I sink into oblivion.

Suddenly I am jolted bolt upright.

"Mrs. Barkman next, please!"

Numb with shock, I try to indicate to the receptionist that all these other people were there first. She dismisses my feeble pleas, takes me firmly by the arm, and steers me down the hall. The temptation to break traces and dash toward the exit is very real, but not quite so overwhelming as the six-foot-four-inch receptionist, who seems to anticipate my every move.

At last we reach the end of a very long hall, negotiate a turn, and come face to face with the chamber of horrors. The sight of a dentist's chair never fails to send shivers down my spine. The receptionist plunks me into it, jams my head between the jaws of the vice, and leaves me to contemplate the instruments of torture.

Alternate waves of nausea and terror sweep across my feeble soul. Nightmarish memories of other years return to haunt me. I remember the day I lost my first baby tooth and three drops of blood gushed from my mouth and stained my best kindergarten dress. The following year I was ever so much braver when a piece of toffee claimed another loose fang. I promptly fainted. By the time I came to, the tooth fairy had left a quarter under my pillow.

Then came the traumatic experience of waiting for two front teeth to appear. Imagining myself doomed to a life of misery as a toothless freak, I examined that gaping hole with a magnifying glass every second day. On alternate days I was sure the teeth would come in crooked, and I would be ridiculed for braces and buck teeth till I was seventy. At last they broke through the gums, relatively straight at that. In the dizzy fit of ecstasy that followed, I almost forgot the toothache that had been developing for days in the vicinity of a hind molar. Eventually it necessitated a trip to the dentist, the first in a long series.

Just the memory of it makes beads of cold sweat form on my brow. At that precise moment the dentist walks in. I panic inwardly. My jaw drops open but no sound escapes. The dreaded gentleman seizes the opportunity, grasps a cant hook, and proceeds to loosen all previous fillings one by one.

With hammer and crowbar he chisels away any remaining enamel. Then while the nerves are still bared, he squirts a jet of ice cold water slowly and methodically into every last tooth. I lift a little higher off the chair with every spurt. Finally I am suspended in mid-air. Casually, the dentist remarks that I have very sensitive teeth.

"Now what seems to be the trouble?" he asks innocently.

At this point, how do I know which one was aching? They all are. I motion in the general direction of a molar. He peers down into the cavernous depths. You'd think he'd never seen a patient's heart in her throat before.

He reaches for the drill. Never mind the freezing. I'm stiff with fear anyway. In rapid succession he bores a series of holes, all converging at a single nerve end. At last he hits bedrock, gives up, and decides to cap the well.

Slowly, oh, so slowly, I start to unwind. My feet are tangled around the footrest. It's like trying to separate two strands of spaghetti. One by one I peel back my fingers from their clenched position.

Now I grope toward that unruly mob in the waiting room. Their turn is yet to come.

When the door finally bangs shut behind me, I am so elated I imagine it to be the first volley in a twenty-one-gun salute. Like a conquering hero, I ride home in victory.

I am barely inside the door when the telephone rings. It seems my neighbor has a toothache. I listen patiently. Coming from an otherwise honest person, her story sounds like an incredible tale of woe. I suggest she make an immediate appointment with her dentist.

"But I'm scared stiff!" she replies.

"Oh, go on! There's not a thing in the world to be afraid of!"

Is that really *me* talking? The very person who but a few hours before was in exactly the same predicament?

What a short memory I have. I can chide our children for being anxious about their school work, forgetting that I was once in that position myself. I can scold our self-conscious teenager, never pausing for a moment to remember my own turbulent years. I can take a dim view of someone else's bad habits, unwilling to admit that I have a few of my own. And here I am impatient with a neighbor, dismissing her fears as being unfounded.

For the sake of others, I must keep reminding myself that some particular victory does not give me liberty to flaunt my triumph before those who are still in the midst of their struggle. Instead it is a golden opportunity to identify with them, encourage them, and be a humble example of God's all-sufficient grace.

3
Dear Diary

Born Again

Knowing that you were not redeemed with perishable things like silver or gold from your futile way of life inherited from your forefathers, but with precious blood, as of a lamb unblemished and spotless, the blood of Christ.

(1 Peter 1:18-19)

Born into Adam's family,
the cord of fellowship with God
was severed by my sins.
So hunger gnawed;
I craved that sip of water
that would quench
my soul's deep thirst.

At last conviction seized me
and squeezed me
and thrust me out
into the understanding
of Your love,
and I was born again
a child of God!

Meditation

There is precious treasure and oil in the dwelling of the wise.

(Proverbs 21:20a)

Meditation—prayerful thinking
As I go about my day,
Resting in His perfect counsel,
Seeking guidance for my way.

Meditation—prayerful thinking
Greets the stranger at my door,
Quiets all complaints of drudgery,
Eases every daily chore.

Meditation—prayerful thinking
In the silence of my soul,
Precious secret of communion,
The success of every goal.

Wishing on Wings

The reward of humility
and the fear of the Lord
Are riches, honor and life.

(Proverbs 22:4)

True to Your Word, whenever I ask
You give me strength for the unknown task;
All the things I seek for body and mind,
You reveal to me and help me find;
But when I knock and the door swings wide
And I catch a glimpse of the wealth inside,
Compared to the treasures You have in store,
The requests I make are little more
Than childish wants—trivial *things*,
Mere wishes mounted on prayerful wings.

The Potter's Wheel

But we have this treasure
in earthen vessels, that the
surpassing greatness of the
power may be of God
and not from ourselves.

(2 Corinthians 4:7)

Except the Lord have mercy
I would be a vessel of dishonor
hardened in the kiln of life.
But in this lump of clay
God saw potential.
I yielded
and on the potter's wheel of time
He's molding me.

Litterbug

*A good name is to be more
desired than great riches,
Favor is better than
silver and gold.*

(Proverbs 22:1)

I was a litterbug
scattering biased opinions
with careless abandon,
accumulating prejudice and pride
in the cobwebs of tradition.
But then Jesus became my Caretaker
and He made a clean sweep!
Oh, I still clutter things up,
but now I grab the broom of confession,
and He whisks my sins
into His dustpan of forgiveness.
Can you see the shine
on a heart swept clean?

Masquerade

To me, the very least of all saints, this grace was given, to preach to the Gentiles the unfathomable riches of Christ, and to bring to light what...has been hidden in God, who created all things.

(Ephesians 3:8-9)

You know, Lord, on this Halloween night
that I feel like a haunted house.
My creaking shell moans and groans
in every wind of adversity.
The cobwebs of prejudice cling to my
    memory,
and the chains of tradition
clank in the empty closets of my soul.

Lord, I confess I'm just a ghost
of what I ought to be.
Forgive me for hiding in the shadows
    of the world,
waiting in vain for tricks or treats.
I want to be a jolly fellow, Lord,
something like the children's jack-o-lantern.
Take me and scoop out the seeds of unbelief,
remove the pulp of materialism,
light Your candle in my hollow soul,
and may Your love cast a mellow glow
in the darkened window of my world.

Wash Line

Thus says the Lord,
'Let not a wise man boast
of his wisdom, and let not the
mighty man boast of his might,
let not a rich man boast of his
riches; but let him who boasts
boast of this, that he
understands and knows Me,
that I am the Lord who
exercises lovingkindness,
justice, and righteousness on
earth; for I delight in these
things,' declares the Lord.

(Jeremiah 9:23-24)

Before the advent of dryers,
Whenever the weather was fine,
Much of the neighborhood gossip
Could be told by the wash on the line.

You knew when the Smiths had their baby
By the flapping of diapers galore,
You could guess at his occupation
By the clothes that the daddy wore.

You could tell when the Sampsons
   had company
By the number of blankets and sheets,
And you knew that the Carters were thrifty
By the patches on trouser seats.

In a world that is constantly changing,
Where values are turned upside down,
For the sake of your neighbor's friendship,
Do you hang out a smile or a frown?

People will size up your habits
As to quality, virtue, and price,
Say, what do you hang on your "clothesline"
That tells the world about Christ?

Fear Not

In this you greatly rejoice, even though now for a little while, if necessary, you have been distressed by various trials, that the proof of your faith, being more precious than gold which is perishable, even though tested by fire, may be found to result in praise and glory and honor at the revelation of Jesus Christ.

(1 Peter 1:6-7)

When some temptation grips my thoughts
And doubts my soul infest,
"Fear not"—faith rallies to the call—
"For God has come to test."
Beyond the reach of circumstance,
Confused, I cannot flee,
But God can open blinded eyes;
"Fear not, stand still, and see."

Though darkness overwhelms my heart
And panic slowly creeps,
"Fear not, the God of Israel
Slumbers not, nor sleeps."
Then morning bursts upon my day,
No need to be afraid:
"He it is that doth go with thee,
Fear thou not, nor be afraid."

Safe Pastures

*The lines have fallen to me
in pleasant places;
Indeed, my heritage is
beautiful to me.*

(Psalm 16:6)

I raced against the Wind
an unbroken stallion
neck arched
nostrils flared
hooves pounding the prairie sod
snorts of alarm
punctuating every encounter
with the One
who sought to tame
my wild rebellion.

Sides heaving
flanks streaked with foam
I sought to quench my thirst
at Springing Waters.
Pausing to drink
I felt His lariat of Love
encircle my life
slip gently down around my will
and lead me gently
Home.

If...

The good man out of the good treasure of his heart brings forth what is good.

(Luke 6:45a)

If I can pierce the hardened hearts of men,
And soften calloused minds
   with tongue or pen,
If I can offer love instead of force
And be a beacon light to souls off course,
If I can lift the burdens of the day
And help to carry loads along the way,
Up heights of grace my steps will lead to God,
And echo back along the pathway trod.

4
Portraits

The Present

Jesus said to him, "If you wish to be complete, go and sell your possessions and give to the poor, and you shall have treasure in heaven; and come, follow Me" (Matthew 19:21).

I was in grade three at the time—too young to know the reasons, but old enough to sense the despair that had settled over our small farming community. Crops had been poor, prices low, and people had become the passive victims of an economic squeeze. The annual school Christmas concert was to be the one and only highlight of an otherwise bleak winter.

To add to the excitement, the new teacher suggested that we draw names for the exchange of gifts. She was probably unaware of the burden that placed upon our young shoulders. I browsed through the Eaton catalog for days before coming to a decision, made all the more difficult because the value of the gift was not to exceed fifty cents.

The names we had chosen were to remain top secret. It didn't take hours, however, for news to spread on the school grapevine. Long before the night of the concert I knew who had drawn my name.

He was a boy from a large family that had just recently moved into our community. Their farm with its derelict buildings was located in an area we referred to locally as "the marsh." In wet years it flooded. In dry years the sandy soil supported some scrub poplars and, at best, a few head of scrawny cattle.

"Don't count too much on a present," my mother cautioned. Caught up in the excitement of the season, I was in no mood for such pessimism.

The night of the concert was clear and cold. A blizzard the day before had packed the rural roads with snowdrifts. As we converged that night upon the village school house, teams of horses stood draped in blankets, their nostrils white with hoarfrost. Those of us who arrived by tractor covered the motors quickly, hopeful that they would start again later for the long ride home.

The school basement was packed. You could smell damp woolen mittens drying on the radiators, and humidity hung heavy in the air. But there in the corner stood the tree in all its glory, the gifts piled high around it. How a bit of wrapping paper can transform the smallest tokens into bits of magic!

The concert got under way as a wide-eyed beginner faltered through a "Welcome" recitation. The stage was made of planks placed across sawhorses, and as the various classes filed up and down to perform their songs, the sound of shuffling feet was accompanied by squeaking boards and a piano thumping out "The Parade of the Wooden Soldiers."

There were skits, drills, and more recitations, with teachers doing the prompting

from behind the bed sheets we used as curtains. A hearty round of applause followed every item, until at last a doll cradle placed in the center of the bare stage indicated the beginning of the nativity pageant. A hush settled over the audience as a youthful scribe began to read from Luke 2: "And it came to pass in those days, that there went out a decree from Caesar Augustus that all the world should be taxed."*

As the curtains closed on the manger scene, the chairman of the school board rose to make closing remarks.

"And have you all been good boys and girls this year?" He cupped his hands to his ears, and a reassuring, "Yes!" echoed from the first few rows of benches, while the teachers nodded in agreement.

Then came the time for which we had all waited—the distribution of gifts.

I sat in suspense, my heart pounding with anticipation. On every side of me people were opening gaily wrapped parcels. There were any number of things to delight a small girl—perfume, soap, trinkets, jewelry. *Surely*, I thought, *my turn will come soon.*

The boy who had drawn my name was opening a cap gun, aiming it at his friends, planning a game of cops and robbers.

I edged over closer to the tree. There were only three presents under it now. Then two. Then none.

I clutched my bag of candies and examined the tree more closely. Maybe my gift was still tucked up there among the branches where nobody could see it.

I tried to be brave as my mother wrapped my coat around my shoulders. I pulled on my mittens and boots. As we stepped outside into the cold prairie night, the tears froze on my cheeks.

How I hated that boy for drawing my name! Hated everything there was about Christmas and celebrating and singing "Joy to the World."

The tractor motor turned over stiffly, hesitated, and then jumped to life, startling the horses around us. I was glad it drowned out the sound of their bells. Stupid things, anyway.

For a long while I sat in silence, until at last the bitterness inside me exploded. "Why did he have to draw my name anyway? I mean, why did he take a name at all?"

"Well," my mother replied gently, "sometimes it's very hard to admit you're poor, even poorer than the rest." I had the feeling she was speaking from experience. "Maybe that boy wanted to give somebody a present just as much as you hoped to get one."

And as we rode home on that starry December night, she began to elaborate on some of the harsh realities of life. I lay on my back in the straw-filled trailer and listened, while the exhaust from the tractor unfurled like a white plume across the sky.

By the time we reached the warmth of home, I had begun to realize that what we get out of life is not so important. The real tragedy is in having nothing to give.

*King James Version.

Tribute to a Rural Mother

Her worth is far above jewels (Proverbs 31:10b).

Mother, God bless her! Somewhere long ago there must have been a springtime in her life, a time when pretty clothes and dates and girlish pleasures thrilled her heart. But somehow that season is so far removed that the image of our mother in that setting is foreign to our mind. Oh, sometimes when she sits and pages through the Eaton's catalog, reminiscing of the styles no longer here, we catch a fleeting glimpse of Mother waiting at the gate for Dad. She is wearing a brown crepe dress with ruffles at the neckline. Suddenly the picture fades, swept away by a thousand and one memories more vivid in our mind.

We see Mother, not in brown crepe and ruffles, but wearing a cotton print housedress and gingham apron. This was the standard uniform of her profession, the dress a reminder that she was never far removed from her responsibilities, the apron signifying she was on active duty.

We see her apron dusty with flour as she greased the ball of bun dough in the kneading pan. We see her gathering eggs and carrying them to the house in her apron. We see Mother in the garden, stooping now and then to tuck a few pods of green peas into her apron pocket. We see her return from the orchard and tumble an apronful of golden crabapples across the kitchen table. And long after the saskatoons had disappeared, we see evidence of that first scant picking staining Mother's apron.

51

Yes, Mother's apron was a homespun symbol of her willingness to cope with any situation, and she never hesitated to use it to that end. When the runt from the litter of pigs was finally shipped triumphantly and tearfully to market, we recalled the morning Mother had carried him home in her apron. Near the warmth of the kitchen stove, he soon revived sufficiently to squeal for lunch, sending us children into gleeful fits of amusement.

Yes, it was the summer of Mother's life, the season when she had to cope with children and with chores, with drought and with depression, with being bone weary and dog tired, and still carrying on—for the sake of the children. We never suspected the real reason she always insisted on walking to town for a few groceries. We thought it was because the roses were blooming at the sandhill or because the pin cherries were ripe or maybe the tiger lilies had opened. So we romped along beside her, unaware that our constant chatter was her therapy and the things of nature a vivid testimony of her belief in the unfailing goodness of God.

Mother had mastered child psychology. She gained our respect not because she demanded it or even asked for it. She deserved it. Her trust in us as children spurred us on to greater heights of achievement. "Do the best you can," she would say, and we did. When the end result was less than we anticipated, the inner assurance that we had tried our hardest was our biggest consolation.

In those harvest days of long ago, Mother always carried lunch to the "men" who were working in the field. Our sagging spirits lifted as we saw her waiting at the corner of the field, her apron spread over the pans of sandwiches and ginger cake, while the coffee steamed from the white enamel pitcher in the stubble by her side.

Time flees. Mother's responsibilities have shifted with the seasons, and Mother herself is in the autumn of her life. Her efforts on our behalf, and she would be the first to admit it, were not always ideal, certainly not perfect, but they were her best. Today we acknowledge them as such and pause to extend our gratitude.

Gathering Eggs with Uncle Jim

But lay up for yourselves treasures in heaven, where neither moth nor rust destroys, and where thieves do not break in or steal; for where your treasure is, there will your heart be also."

(Matthew 6:20-21)

You needed at least three baskets to gather eggs with Uncle Jim. It wasn't that he kept such a large flock. Two dozen hens couldn't possibly lay *that* many eggs, even if they were as pampered as Uncle Jim's. And besides, hens lay only once a day. Uncle Jim and I went gathering eggs at least three times daily. Sometimes four.

"I think it's about time to gather eggs again, don't you?" was Uncle Jim's invitation to go exploring about the farmyard. Strangely enough, the offer was usually extended at the precise time a sudden wave of homesickness threatened to engulf me.

Gathering up our baskets we would start off in the direction of the barn. In the bottom of one basket were carrots for the small Angora rabbit. Snowflake was so white and soft I was sure she would melt the minute I touched her.

Angus, on the other hand, was a big black Aberdeen bull, as solid and shiny as a chunk of onyx. When he rolled his eyes at me I could never, ever, summon up enough courage to feed him the goodies from my basket. Uncle Jim would chuckle as he placed some cabbage leaves in the manger. "What's the matter? Angus making eyes at you again?"

I was only too happy to move on with my basket and dole out its treasures to Millie and Mollie and Flossie and Pet. I knew for a fact *they* appreciated my handouts. Didn't they always reward me with foaming pails of milk? I have always associated the sleepy whine of the cream separator with life on Uncle Jim's farm.

Next we would pay a visit to the pigpen. Now here was *real* appreciation! The pigs' manners were a bit lacking in finesse, but their gratitude was genuine. The dust from the chopped grain adhered to their eyelashes like white mascara, and I pictured how they would look wearing poke bonnets.

On to the chicken house, where we emptied out the basket of potato peelings. I was de-

lighted to discover that a tardy hen had left an unexpected egg in one of the far nests. It still felt warm to the touch, and I cupped it in my hand, reluctant to expose this miracle of God to the cold hard ribbing of my wicker basket.

We would take the long way back to the house, sauntering along the orchard path, picking a golden apple here and there, checking to see if the plums were ripe. At dusk we would pause at the "turkey tree," as Uncle Jim called it. He claimed it grew turkeys every evening about this time. Their black shapes clung to the limbs of the gnarled old willow like giant blights.

As we strolled along the edge of the garden, Uncle Jim would pick a few choice tomatoes or maybe some lettuce, while I fished under the leaves of the cucumber patch for the big ones.

By the time we reached the veranda, our baskets contained quite an assortment of fruits and vegetables, and Aunt Emma would chide us gently. "I thought you two went to gather the eggs."

"We did." Uncle Jim's eyes would twinkle with amusement as he unloaded our baskets. If all else failed, he could always produce the porcelain nest egg that he carried in his pocket for just such an emergency.

I have thought back many times to those childhood excursions around Uncle Jim's farm. Over the years I have met my share of "Snowflakes"—shy people who seemed to melt into the woodwork whenever I reached out in their direction. The "carrots" I used to befriend them ranged anywhere from a cup of coffee to a full meal, and they responded with gentle trust.

At the same time there were the big stubborn Angus kind of people, who tried to bully me and then had the nerve to roll their eyes in dismay when I stopped short of being a doormat.

But those are few and far between. As if to compensate, there are always those people who respond awkwardly but enthusiastically to the smallest token of love. What an unexpected miracle to find a bouquet of flowers on my doorstep, left there by that crusty old woman who lives up the street! I wish I could preserve it forever as a symbol of what one small kindness can do. Whoever dreamed she would appreciate that ride to the store so much?

As time goes on, I realize my "basket" contains quite an assortment of "treasures"— friends and acquaintances whose lives became involved with mine through some small effort made on their behalf. As life spreads out to encompass a wider range of interests, I'm beginning to feel that Uncle Jim left behind him a unique legacy. In order to lay up treasures in heaven we need at least three baskets. That way we are always prepared with something to give, provided with something to gather, and blessed with something to keep.

The Valentine

Precious in the sight of the Lord
Is the death of His godly ones (Psalm 116:15).

"Can you come," she said, "and help me make a valentine?"

It was an unusual request under the circumstances, and yet her voice conveyed a sense of urgency.

As I drove across town that night I wondered how anyone who had suffered from bone cancer for three long years could possibly muster up enough courage to make valentines.

Her husband greeted me at the door of their cozy bungalow, a tea towel in his hand. I noticed for the first time that his hair was beginning to gray around the temples and that his shoulders slumped forward in perpetual weariness. Although he never complained, the demands upon him were beginning to tell.

I went into the bedroom where his wife was propped up by pillows on a bed cluttered with ribbons, paper doilies, and red construction paper. She greeted me as she always did, asking about our family, showing me her latest "Keep Cheer" cards, praising the thoughtful people who had sent them. A friend had given her a pink satin bed jacket and she insisted on modeling it for me, even though she cried out in pain as her husband gently moved her forward in order to slip it around her shoulders.

She looked lovely, and we told her so. For a moment she basked in the attention and then with a broad grin, said, "All right, you two. Flattery won't do. We've got work to get finished." She handed me a piece of red paper and a pair of scissors.

"Jerry, you go and make the coffee."

For the next few minutes we sketched and cut and pasted hearts together like a couple of schoolgirls assembling valentines for their current boyfriends. We laughed and reminisced and engaged in cheerful banter with her husband out in the kitchen. "Jerry, how do you spell Philippians?"

We could hear him paging through the Bible before calling out the answer. "One *l* and two *p*'s."

"He's gotta be kidding!" she exclaimed in mock horror. "Quick, give me that eraser before he comes!"

57

Their boys, meanwhile, were deeply engrossed in a new game and protested loudly when their father summoned them to bed. A few minutes later, however, the youngest fellow shuffled in and dropped to his knees at his mother's bedside, not the least bit self-conscious about saying his prayers in my presence.

The house grew quiet now, and I could hear the coffee gurgling in the pot. We put the finishing touches on the valentine, and Thelma sank back into the pillows, exhausted, but with a smile of satisfaction curving across lines drawn straight by pain.

A week later at midnight we received the call. "This is Jerry. I want you to know that Thelma passed away an hour ago. That's all I can say at the moment. Good night."

The message was brief but striking in its simplicity.

In the hours that followed, my mind flashed back to the last time I had heard her sing. We were holding an afternoon service at a local nursing home, and she insisted on helping with the music. In a clear soprano, she led a mixed quartet as we sang, "I've found a Friend; oh, such a Friend!" Unable to stand throughout all five verses, she reluctantly agreed to sing from her wheelchair, one invalid inspiring countless others.

On the day of the funeral the sorrowful young family followed the coffin slowly up the aisle, a bereaved husband and two sons, the grieving father with a hand on each boy's shoulder. At the sight of that sad little procession the entire congregation wept with compassion, and we dabbed at our eyes with wet hankies.

When I finally looked up, the ladies' choir had filed into place. There was a conspicuous vacancy in the center row, second from the right.

At the close of the service I stood at her coffin for a moment to pay last respects. She looked beautiful, loose curls framing her face, a faint smile captured at the corner of her lips. I was suddenly aware that her cherished verse had become a reality: "The Lord is my strength and my shield; my heart trusted in Him, and I am helped: therefore my heart greatly rejoiceth; and with my song will I praise him" (Psalm 28:7, KJV).

Somewhere in southern Manitoba an elderly couple has a box filled with priceless keepsakes. Among them is a simple homemade valentine from their beloved Thelma, sent to them the very week she died. At the bottom, in her own handwriting, is the following benediction: "The peace of God, which passeth all understanding, shall keep your hearts and minds through Christ Jesus. Phil. 4:7."

Thelma fought the good fight, she finished the course, she kept the faith. There is laid up for her that eternal treasure, the crown of righteousness promised in 2 Timothy 4:8.

5
Keepsakes

The Solitaire

And I will give you the treasures of darkness,
And hidden wealth of secret places (Isaiah 45:3a).

*H*ouses come and houses go, but the old outhouse has retained its Spartan lines, a familiar piece of architecture on the rural landscape.

Though called a dozen different names, most of which are unprintable, prairie dwellers will recognize at once the trademarks of a genuine model: the gray weatherbeaten exterior peppered with knotholes, the jagged half moon carved in the sagging door, the shanty roof bared defiantly to the elements. Over the years, the prairie winds had forced the whole structure to lean slightly back on its haunches. To postpone the inevitable, or maybe as a necessary precaution against Halloween pranksters, the House of Parliament was propped up behind by a couple of poplar poles.

The location of the outhouse in relation to the other buildings was entirely dependent upon the constitution of its owner. I have, on occasion, visited those that were but a few steps removed from the back porch. Almost too late, I have discovered that others were far enough removed from civilization to necessitate a brisk two-minute walk. The usual site was a spot somewhere between the two extremes.

Regardless of location, the furnishings were always basic to the purpose for which the outhouse was intended. You twisted the swivel button on its rusty nail, the door creaked open, and you lifted it into place behind you. Privacy was secured with the aid of a wire hook made out of an old clothes hanger. It had scratched a perfect arc in the board to which it was fastened, the depth of the engraving being some indication of the building's age.

A shaft of yellow sunlight peered through a knothole, illuminating the cobwebs draped from every corner. Beside you was an ample supply of obsolete newspapers and the second last Eaton's catalog. As a child you probably peered down the other hole and realized it was a long way down. Or vice versa.

As time marched on, the outhouses boasted a few local improvements. The shanty style gave way to a peak roof and the half moon in the door became diamond shaped. There was even a store-bought hook and a spring that snapped the door shut behind you, thereby confirming the necessity of your trip. The place smelled of creosote disinfectant, and there was a real roll of toilet paper hanging on a wire holder.

The ultramodern ones even had a light bulb, once you found it in the dark. It hung from the ceiling by its twisted wire and was powered by the farm's 32-watt generator. The moths ticked against its feeble light, and you ducked for the big ones.

I remember sloshing through the water in spring and breaking the crusts of ice from around the puddles. The floor of the outhouse was covered with muddy footprints;

the rain dripped down from the eaves and trickled in around the cracks. The dead leaves in the corner soaked it up until they were a sodden mass, but outside the first pussy willows brushed softly against the roof.

Come summer, you dawdled along the path until the mosquitoes swarmed up gray before you, and with flailing arms you ran the last few steps, grateful for the relative protection of the outhouse. Safe within, you could hear your tormentors seeking their revenge. A shiny black beetle crawled about the floor, and you amused yourself by blocking its movements with your big toe. A red squirrel skittered across the roof, scolding you for intruding on his domain.

And then it was fall. The smell of harvest was in the air. The leaves were turning color and spiraling to the ground. A few of them found their way into the old outhouse, along with an acorn or two. In the corner, a shallow box with a B.C. fruit label contained a fresh supply of peach-scented paper. An enterprising mouse—or was it the squirrel?—had chewed the cover of the spring and summer catalog, which had only recently expired.

But then came winter, and who but a martyr could forget those memorable trips to the outhouse in the middle of January? Blowing against the frost on the kitchen window, you squinted through the little peephole and decided whether you could make it over the snowbanks or whether you would have to allow enough time to shovel a path.

The door of the outhouse strained against a snowdrift as you squeezed yourself in. The bare branches of the willow scratched and clawed at the roof. Wisps of snow swirled around your feet. And then came the ultimate test of courage: you took a deep, deep breath and sat down on the hoarfrosted seat.

Spring, summer, fall, and winter, the stoic old outhouse stood its ground, as one person after another sought asylum within the privacy of its four board walls. Because the call of nature was an accepted part of daily life, no one ever questioned the propriety of your visits. Consequently the outhouse became an oasis for the exiled, where, far removed from the critical stares of the family, a 4-H club member could wax eloquent on his prepared speech, or a dreamy-eyed teenager could pore over the tender contents of that first love letter. It was the place, too, where the laggard student could cram for tests at the last possible moment or bone up on current events, courtesy of the weekly paper. And many a young musician, banished for practicing his harmonica indoors, simply removed himself out to the ready-made studio, where he continued to play with undiminished enthusiasm.

It was a place where time stood still, where, totally immune from distractions, you could either concentrate on the urgent or languish in a brief respite from all responsibility, whatever was most necessary at the moment. Either way, you discovered the "hidden wealth of secret places"—the value of being totally alone, of setting yourself aside for those personal needs that were strictly your own, no excuses needed.

6
Jewels, Precious Jewels

City Kids and Country Cows

How blessed is the man who finds wisdom
And the man who gains understanding.
For its profit is better than the profit of silver,
And its gain than fine gold (Proverbs 3:13-14).

I have barely gulped down the last of my tuna fish sandwich when Junior announces it is time to go to school. I am to accompany his suburban kindergarten class on their first visit to a farm.

The teacher is a pert young thing who is not a bit disturbed by the antics of her young charges. Forty-seven angels and not a halo in the bunch! Horrors! I'd go berserk in two days with that kind of responsibility.

I see a few other mothers have also been conscripted for this particular outing. It must be their first visit to a farm as well. They are wearing sandals. White ones.

The teacher calls the roll. Anonymous heads pop up in response to their names. I am to choose six and board the waiting school bus. They scramble on ahead of me, and all dive for the same seat. I get them untangled only to discover I no longer have the original six. I believe I have lost two and added three, or is it the other way around? Well, no matter. The teacher assures me they are all there. I just wonder if I am.

The noise is deafening.

"Lookit! Lookit! Lookit!" They look at *every-thing*. Not only that, but they expect me to do the same. I begin to feel as if my head is swiveling on a universal joint.

A few miles down the road, somebody spies a lone horse standing beside a straw stack. "Here we are! There's the dairy farm!"

As the bus rolls right on by, our young tour guide quickly accounts for his mistake. "Well, it sure *smelled* like one."

At last the bus rambles down the gravel road to the farm. First stop, the pig barns.

"Phew!"

"That's even worse than my big brother's socks!"

"Boy, that mama pig is fat. Does she eat lots and lots?"

"Sure. That's how come she's a pig."

"You don't have to say it so loud. See, she's looking right at you."

64

The offender squirms a bit under mama pig's scrutiny. "When can we see the cows?"

We trek along to the next enclosure. The teacher explains that these are beef cattle, "boy cows."

Somebody discovers the grand-daddy of them all reclining in his stall. He rolls his eyes at the throng of young visitors, and they stare back in open-mouthed amazement. The teacher takes advantage of the silence. "Now, boys and girls, this is the daddy cow. Can anyone tell me what he's called?"

"Elmer?" suggests a timid voice from the crowd.

It's about time for milking, so we troop along to the dairy barn. One adventuresome young fellow wants to take a shortcut.

"Don't go through there!" shouts a little girl. "That's where the cows go to the bathroom."

"It is not! They go right in the barn!"

"Maybe *your* cows do, but *mine* aren't going to!"

A very optimistic student, that one.

The holsteins gaze at us with interest.

"Look, teacher, they're all chewing gum!" The whole class becomes absorbed in watching this strange phenomenon while teacher explains all about cuds.

Suddenly a cow does the unpardonable. She moos. Right in somebody's ear.

The poor little kid is so terrified he almost creates a stampede among his classmates. Everybody is hanging on to me for dear life. "Is it gonna moo again? Huh, Mrs. Bark-man, is it?"

I try to reassure them.

"But that one's getting mad. She's switching her tail."

"Oh, but that's to keep the flies away."

He isn't so sure. "I don't see any flies. Do you?" (It's a very automated farm, you see. Disinfected and all.)

"Let's just be quiet and watch the milking."

At this point they are not quite sure which end merits the most attention, the noise-maker or the dairy bar. Truly a cow is an amazing machine.

"Does she make chocolate milk too?"

"Don't be silly!" replies a classmate. "This isn't a brown cow."

I explain that all cows give white milk.

"Then how come some chickens lay brown eggs?"

I am glad the teacher interrupts at this point. It is time to board the bus.

Mightily inspired by this new adventure, we sing umpteen verses of "Old MacDonald Had a Farm." He has just added a very vocal billy goat to his menagerie when the bus pulls up at school, thus ending lesson one on bovine behavior, kindergarten level.

If I think back far enough, I, too, can remember being intrigued by the habits of farm animals, but when I went to school I got the impression that cows were "kid stuff," that big people didn't waste time marveling at nature. And so for years, cows were nothing more than props on the prairie landscape.

One of motherhood's most rewarding experiences, however, is the excuse it affords us to look at life once more through the eyes of a child. In our haste to attain maturity, we sometimes abandon too many of our child-like qualities—the joy of discovery, the keen powers of observation, the total acceptance of God as Creator. What once came natural-ly now requires a conscious effort on our part.

Some of the world's most delightful people are those who are not self-conscious about their "childish" interests. You'll find them at the playground on the swings or building sand castles with their grandchildren at the beach. They are the people who seem to be on talking terms with the animals at the zoo, and who can coax birds and squirrels to eat from their hand. They are the people who are unabashedly eager to go on picnics, to explore new places, to try their hand at new skills. They may not have much in material goods, but they have gained insight that is infinitely more satisfying than any-thing money could buy. They are rich in understanding.

The Winner!

"I walk in the way of righteousness,
In the midst of the paths of justice,
To endow those who love me with wealth,
That I may fill their treasuries" (Proverbs 8:20-21).

If by age six you have already learned to blame your gardening failures on the weather, you are definitely a prospective member of the local horticultural society. A *very* optimistic bunch, they are not going to let you be discouraged if the weeds choke out your first crop of carrots or if the zinnias are not in the best of bloom. There is still a competition open for you at the local fair: "Enter the model contest, making either birds, animals, people, etc., using any combination of fruit, flowers, vegetables, leaves, roots, or shrub branches."

I may not be raising any outstanding gardeners, but I have toted off to the fair some ingenious masterpieces to be entered in the above category. I am proud to say that I am the first mother whose son jumped right up into the Court of Honor via the "Celebrated Jumping Frog." He made it out of cucumbers, and it perched on a big rock against the velvet backdrop surrounded by blooms of every description. A very arresting sight.

The following year he entered a "Monster Mosquito," no doubt inspired by the many at large. The judges got the point—he again captured first prize.

Let me remind you that such honors are not easily forthcoming. Before ever reaching the exhibit hall, one must anticipate all sorts of catastrophes. The frog, for instance, kept losing a hind leg, and I had to take along spare cucumbers for replacement parts. The proboscis on the monster mosquito was in reality the long pointed root of a slender carrot, and I had to guard the thing with my life for fear it would snap off and ruin the whole idea.

This year was no exception. Our youngest fellow dreamed up a lady made out of rhubarb stalks, with a green tomato head and a zinnia hat. We dubbed her "Rhubarb Rosie," and she proved to be quite a celebrity even before she made her debut at the fair.

I put her in the back seat and cautioned her young escort to treat her as a gentleman should. Before long, however, he was entertaining passing motorists by holding her up for their inspection.

Then it happened. Her head fell off and she lost a green pea eye. In the excitement that followed, somebody squashed the pea and such wails arose from the back seat that I was forced to the curb to restore order. No, I didn't have any peas along in my purse. Yes, we would drive home for a pod. No, we won't be late. Yes, I'm sure she will win a prize.

And so five miles and ten minutes later, Rhubarb Rosie arrived intact at the horticultural fair. She may not have been much to look at, but she was the prize of one small boy, age six, prospective gardener, keen competitor, and all-around good citizen.

Hospitals Make Me Sick

A faithful envoy brings healing (Proverbs 13:17b).

He is five. He eats like a chicken, growls like a bear, and snores like a trooper. The doctor confirms my diagnosis: he is to have his tonsils removed, the sooner the better.

Once surgery is slated, the neighbors are all helpful, especially the smaller ones. "I had my tonsils out once. The doctor just cuts your head off, picks them out, and then sews it back on. See, here's even the mark."

It turns out to be a cat scratch.

The adults are much more encouraging. One even brings him a book entitled *Goodbye Tonsils*. It's a nice little tale about all the nice little things that happen to you at hospitals. Very delicately written.

Our five-year-old victim is suspect. "I don't want to hear it."

Oh, well, ignorance is bliss, or is it?

"What happens if the doctor runs out of thread when he's sewing me up?"

"Oh, but he doesn't sew you up when he takes your tonsils out."

"How does he do it then?"

"He reaches down your throat with a sharp pair of scissors."

"What if he misses and pokes my eye out? Will I grow a new one?"

"No, dear, you can't grow a new eye, but the doctor won't miss. Doctors don't make mistakes."

"But you told me everybody makes mistakes sometimes."

I didn't really expect my philosophical teachings would come home to roost at age five. I suggest we go for a walk.

"Are we going to the hospital right now?"

It's a question I've answered in the negative quite often during the last three weeks, but today is the day.

As the hospital looms into sight, he becomes apprehensive. "Can I suck my thumb?"

I park the car. He looks around curiously. "If I get killed, where do they bury me?"

I hasten to reassure him, but he has evidently come to grips with the possibility. "Oh, well, as long as they cut my heart out and send it up to God, I'll be OK. Right, Mom?"

He strides manfully up the steps, his pillow under one arm and a stuffed dog under the other. A fellow has to be prepared, you know. Even at that your emotions can get the best of you. Just as we reach the door, he bursts into tears, which in turn set off a coughing spell.

The admitting clerk is understanding. "If he's coming down with a cold we have to cancel surgery, you know." Just like that.

I assure her he's not, but she remains dubious. As a mere mother, I hate to argue while standing there in the foyer of the hospital. I feel I have no grounds for defense.

At last a wise nurse takes command of the situation. The patient blows his nose, wipes his tears, takes a firm grip on his toy dog, and proceeds on schedule.

He eyes his new surroundings with suspicion, convinced, I'm sure, that behind every door there lurks a nurse with an itchy needle finger. At last he delves into the toy box.

"When do I get something to eat?"

"At suppertime."

"Can I have two helpings?" It's a sure sign he's settling in. The clock ticks on.

Visiting hours are over. I tuck him in. "It's time for me to leave now. You're a big boy, and all the nice nurses will be here to look after you."

He nods his head solemnly. A tear rolls slowly down his cheek.

As I get into the car I keep thinking that a city hospital is a huge place in which to leave such a little boy, alone. Funny I never noticed the mist on my glasses till now.

It's a long night. At 3:00 A.M. I resist the impulse to phone the children's ward and ask if he's sleeping. Nurses are notorious liars anyhow when it comes to dealing with distraught mothers.

I'm up at the crack of dawn. One hour. Wonder if he's awake. Two hours. Wonder if he's crying. Three hours. I scrape the ice from the windshield and take off.

I'm not supposed to see him prior to surgery. "Too emotionally disturbing" is how they explained it when I protested. Frankly, if I'm ever slated for the scalpel I want all the moral support I can muster, regardless of what anybody says.

As I step out of the elevator, the nurses regard me with cold stares. *Another spoiled mother who can't refrain from interfering. Doesn't she know her son is perfectly OK?*

That's strictly professional opinion. Any mother worth the title knows that a child who is thrust into a strange world is not "perfectly OK." Especially when he's sitting in his bed, crying. Hospitals make me sick.

We talk of his impending operation, and I reassure him. We read books together. We watch TV. He has a bath. He is highly indignant that he has to wear a nightgown. That's girl stuff.

He gets a needle. A man comes to wheel him to the operating room. He's dressed in green. "From Mars, maybe?"

As they go down the hall together I hear the patient reassuring himself. "My mommy's going to be waiting for me when I get back."

You bet I am, sonny.

The minutes stretch into hours. At last the doctor comes in. "He's in the recovery room. Everything went fine, but his tonsils were enormous, simply enormous. Should have had them bronzed and put on the mantle."

Now that's what I admire in a doctor. A good sense of humor *after* the ordeal, not *before* it.

The patient returns intact. His favorite pillow is at the foot of the bed—in a garbage bag. It has followed him to the thick of the battle, and then in the recovery room he throws up on it. History has recorded worse casualties during a retreat.

At this point our hero couldn't care less. "I'm thirsty," he squeaks. I tank him up with water. His stomach promptly revolts. He sinks back onto his bed and sleeps.

All of a sudden it hits me: the tonsils are out, and I'm all in. Nervous exhaustion, they call it. Hospital syndrome, peculiar to motherhood.

If any gift is to be particularly treasured, it is the gift of health. Those of us who have seldom been called upon to suffer cannot fully comprehend the anguish of illness; consequently we may take our health for granted to such an extent that we are actually guilty of neglecting the "temple of God" in which we live. The other extreme is to place health on such a pedestal as to elevate it *beyond* the will of God.

Young mothers are particularly subject to these two extremes. With all the demands upon them, it is relatively easy to ignore their own health requirements while attending to those of the family. The conscientious mother who is overly concerned about her baby's welfare may disregard the fact that she is sacrificing her own health in the process and thus depriving them both.

It is not easy (and sometimes seemingly impossible) to get sufficient rest and eat a balanced diet when there are small children in the house. There were times I thought I would faint from sheer exhaustion and collapse in a heap at the bottom of the stairs while on my way to put yet another load of diapers in the wash. The human body is particularly resilient, however. A quick nap here, a snack there, and I was sufficiently refreshed to carry on for the time being.

The danger is in believing that we can do this year in and year out and suffer no ill effects. "Do you not know that you are the temple of God" (1 Corinthians 3:16)? In the interests of economy alone it is not wise to keep patching up a building whose foundations are crumbling. Better to do a complete renovation of habits than to risk the loss of health, "for the temple of God is holy, and that is what you are" (1 Corinthians 3:17b).

There is, however, the other extreme, that of placing physical health and healing above and beyond that which is spiritually beneficial. Just as great cathedrals and thatched huts can both be designated as places of worship, so God chooses to dwell in both the robust and the frail. Who is to say which "temple" is the more useful? Did Christ not forgo the "ivory palaces" to serve in a "land of woe"?

Although it is *natural* to want the best of everything from God, including health, it is *supernatural* to serve Him despite our afflictions. "My strength," says God, "is made perfect in weakness" (2 Corinthians 12:9, KJV). To virtually demand His healing touch may be a selfish effort to erect "cathedrals" where God wants "thatched huts." Both have their place in His kingdom.

I have heard outstanding testimonies about the God who dwells in all sorts of "temples," and whether in sickness or in health, we are His "peculiar treasure," envoys sent to bring spiritual healing to those around us.

7
Snapshots

Day One

And he shall be the stability of your times, A wealth of salvation, wisdom, and knowledge; The fear of the Lord is his treasure.

(Isaiah 33:6)

I watched the school bus gobble up
Its victims one by one;
Like some gigantic predator
It even ate *my* son!
It hypnotized its innocent prey
With bright and flashing eye,
It swallowed children whole
Before they even waved good-bye.

Though burdened with their textbooks
Symbolic of their call,
These martyrs of curriculum
Still dreamed of playing ball.
I marveled at the carefree way
Such heroes met their fate,
And there I stood, a weakling,
Crying at the gate!

Knitting

That their hearts may be encouraged, having been knit together in love, and attaining to all the wealth that comes from the full assurance of understanding, resulting in a true knowledge of God's mystery, that is, Christ Himself, in whom are hidden all the treasures of wisdom and knowledge.

(Colossians 2:2-3)

When life's not a ball but a tangled skein,
We can't break it off and start over again,
But we have to knit with the yarn we've got,
Whether we like it or not.

Begin by casting your care upon Him
And proceed in faith when directions dim,
For we're often surprised, if we don't give up,
How things look differently, right side up.

If you drop a stitch, be quick to confess,
For the longer you go, the bigger the mess!
Splice any breaks with the utmost care
and cover the knots with silent prayer.

If you gauge your work it will be just right,
Things not slack, nor tension tight.
Follow the patterns found in the Book,
But rest your eyes with an upward look.

Repeat every row, God's leading obey
As you take up your knitting, day after day.
You'll find, in time, your worries decrease;
In direct proportion, your blessings increase.

God's Bouquet

Instruct them to do good,
to be rich in good works,
to be generous and ready to
share, storing up for themselves
the treasure of a good
foundation for the future,
so that they may take hold of
that which is life indeed.

(1 Timothy 6:18-19)

Our life is a floral arrangement,
Container, color, and line
Focused on goals we have chosen,
Filled in with the details fine.

God admires the lines of simplicity,
He treasures a single bloom,
Enhanced by the service we offer,
Our talents—enriching perfume.

We may need the spikes of affliction
The thorns of a burden to bear,
Or a shadowy cluster of sorrows
To set off some beauty rare.

God cultivates, plucks, and arranges
An infinite number of flowers,
Selecting the buds and shaping our lives,
A bouquet of golden hours.

Thanksgiving Garden

The Lord shall open unto thee his good treasure, the heaven to give the rain unto thy land in its season, and to bless all the work of thine hand.

(Deuteronomy 28:12, KJV)

Tomatoes bending low in clusters red,
Symbolic of the sacred blood Christ shed,
Peas forming perfect pearls in emerald rows,
Like promises a loving God bestows,
Carrots penetrating stubborn sod
As piercing as the changeless Word of God,
Potatoes nudged into the light, still smudged
  with earth,
Like human lives that undergo new birth,
Golden ears of corn all swathed in green,
Inner beauty waiting to be seen—
Yes, harvest is a season set apart,
Thanksgiving falls today—within *my* heart.

Why Christmas?

But God, being rich in mercy, because of His great love with which He loved us, even when we were dead in our transgressions, made us alive together with Christ....For by grace you have been saved through faith; and that not of yourselves, it is the gift of God.

(Ephesians 2:4, 5, 8)

Mankind
standing hunched together
like Christmas trees on city parking lots
with a sign above saying
For Sale—Cheap.

Trees
severed from their roots
are bought and carried home,
decorated with cheap ornaments
and artificial snow,
the center of attraction
for a week, or maybe two.
But as the Christmas spirit wears away
the tree is stripped and burned.

Men
cut off from God by sin
are bought by Satan
and for a while they glory
in the show windows of the world,
adorned by the baubles of fame or fortune.
At last, men too are stripped of imitation,
and cast into the fire of condemnation:
"the wages of sin is death."

Why Christmas then?
It is a gift of love,
redemption wrapped in swaddling clothes
and laid in a manger
for the benefit of men sold out to sin.
It is a gift to be accepted or rejected,
the gift of everlasting life
addressed: "From God
To *whosoever* believeth in Him."

Silent Things

Better is a little
  with the fear of the Lord,
Than great treasure
  and turmoil with it.

(Proverbs 15:16)

The taste of honey fresh from the comb,
The earthy smell of new plowed loam,
The delicate quiver of feathery plume,
Ethereal fragrance of rose perfume,
Humor dancing in twinkling eye,
Trees silhouetted against the sky—
While in heartfelt praise the psalmist *sings*,
The giving of thanks for the quiet things
Like a wisp of smoke on the autumn air
Is wafted upward in silent prayer.

Valley of Shadows

How precious is Thy lovingkindness, O God! And the children of men take refuge in the shadow of Thy wings.

(Psalm 36:7)

In the valley of the shadows
We walk by faith, not sight;
There is purpose in His leading
And beyond the darkness, Light.

In the twilight of each sorrow
Is the comfort we call hope;
In the peace of every promise
Can be found the strength to cope.

For at night we rest our burdens
That we bear along the way,
Cast on Him our every heartache
And await the break of day.

Harbor of Prayer

For there is no distinction between Jew and Greek; for the same Lord is Lord of all, abounding in riches for all who call upon Him.

(Romans 10:12)

There is nearby a sheltered cove
Where billows cease to roar;
Its beauty is reflected
By the lights along the shore.
All those marooned by circumstance
Or shipwrecked by a storm,
Find shelter, yes, and comfort, too,
And fellowship that's warm.
But faith alone can fathom
The depth of blessings there
In the peaceful tides that linger
Round the harbor some call *prayer.*

50 Memory Lane

By wisdom a house is built,
And by understanding
  it is established;
And by knowledge
  the rooms are filled
With all precious
  and pleasant riches.

(Proverbs 24:3)

There's a grand old house down
    Memory Lane
On the right-hand side of the street.
It was built with love and sacrifice
At the place where two paths meet.
The shady boughs of a gnarled old tree
Still spread their branches above
The spacious lawn where children played
In a yard hedged in with love.

The veranda is covered with trailing vines
Like memories all entwined,
And the quiet faith of the folks inside
Is marked by a sentinel pine.
There's a winding path leading up
  to the door
To the point where two lives merged,
And a welcome mat and a well-worn sill
Where countless steps converged.

It's fifty years since that grand old house
Took shape in a couple's dreams,
And they stepped across its threshold
But yesterday, it seems.
And the grand old house became a home
Inspiring love and respect,
And the couple strolling down Memory Lane
Claim God was the Architect.

Easter Every Day

Let the word of Christ richly dwell within you, with all wisdom teaching and admonishing one another with psalms and hymns and spiritual songs, singing with thankfulness in your hearts to God.

(Colossians 3:16)

Faith rolled away the stone of unbelief
that sealed my heart in darkness.
Dazzled by the sudden Light
I staggered to its Source
and morning dawned within my soul.

Now standing in the shelter of the cross
I see a ray of hope
that penetrates the tomb:
This shroud of sin that bound me
in the grave,

Christ wore;
The fear of death that shackled me for life,
He overcame.

Praise God!
It's Easter *every* day!

8
Travel Memoirs

A Visit to Grandpa's

Guard...the treasure which has been entrusted to you (2 Timothy 1:14).

Over the sand hill, down across the old red bridge, around the corner, and the clump of poplars that sheltered Grandpa's homestead came into view.

As we turned up the lane after a spring shower, I could look back from the rumble seat of the Model A roadster and watch the tire marks unraveling in the damp sand. Arriving at the muddy stretch of road, we would park the car, don our rubber boots, and walk the last quarter mile.

The sound of voices sifting through the poplars alerted the whole farmyard. A horse whinnied. Off in the distance we could hear a door bang, and the friendly old collie dog came bounding down the lane. Not far behind him was the tom turkey, gobbling a greeting as he trotted out to meet us. As if suddenly mindful of the protocol befitting a bird of his dignity, he would turn abruptly and declare himself our official escort, strutting along in front of us with tail spread wide.

The poplars gradually dwindled, and we were into the clearing. The weatherbeaten frame house stood on a slight knoll overlooking a scattering of granaries and chicken coops. Off to the right was the log barn and a small corral, the top railing worn smooth from the many grandchildren who used it as their pretend pony.

As we drew near the house I instinctively waited for Jack to come and greet me. Jack was a giant afghan-greyhound mixture of dog who loved children. Despite the name, Jack gave birth quite regularly to a motley litter of pups.

"Pa, you oughta give that dog a different name," Grandma would say. "It confuses the young 'uns."

Whereupon Grandpa would chuckle and remind her that Jack knew what "he" was about, even if the rest of us didn't.

I sat out in the summer kitchen playing with Jack's pups while the older folks visited. Before long I would hear the squeak of the back door as Grandma went out to the icehouse for some "vittles." I always tagged along out of curiosity.

Not far from the back step, a big old maple tree provided the one bit of shade in the otherwise open clearing. Under its sprawling roots was Grandma's icehouse. On a blistering hot day I loved an excuse to descend the rickety steps into that cool, dark hideaway. The smell of damp sawdust mingled with the tang of sour cream and smoked ham.

Grandma gathered what she needed from the various crocks sitting about at random and then filled her apron with a dozen or more brown eggs from the wicker basket on the dirt floor.

Before long we would be seated around her large oak table. The red checkered oilcloth was worn white at the edges from the elbows of many visitors. Lunch was usually homemade bread and butter, wild plum jam, and a huge platter of fried eggs, done sunny-side up. I always sat where I could watch the blue willow clock, intrigued by the pendulum as it swung back and forth beneath the hexagonal face with its myriad designs.

Afterwards I joined Grandpa as he retired to his favorite spot at the end of the sagging couch. The crazy quilt that helped compensate for broken springs smelled like horses. It was made out of heavy overcoat patches outlined in a red wool featherstitch, a design that reminded me of the old turkey's footprints in the mud.

After a few minutes of visiting had elapsed, Grandpa would commission me to go to the green buffet and bring him the sugar bowl that he kept hidden behind the mantle clock. It was filled with round white peppermints.

As we sat there with bulging cheeks we could look out the south window to where the vultures hovered over the dugout, their flight patterns handicapped by an enormous meal of lizards. I shuddered at the thought, telling myself I must eat no more than two peppermints, even if Grandpa coaxed me. He told me about other birds that visited the dugout, small ones that bobbed up and down as they walked. "Teeter-bum-snipes" he called them.

Every so often Grandpa leaned ahead slightly, squinting out the opposite window in the direction of the north pasture. That was where the "blue" cow grazed. She had a notorious reputation for jumping fences, and Grandpa liked to keep constant vigil over her behavior from his spot on the end of the couch.

On occasion he would lose sight of her. That was valid enough excuse to swing into the saddle of his sorrel mare and go off with his dogs for an afternoon's fox hunt.

At such times I wandered out to play with Jack's whimpering puppies, or gathered wild roses at the sand hill, or picked saskatoons behind the corral, milking them into a gallon syrup pail.

But that was long ago.

Where once the berries hung in purple clusters and the wind whispered through the poplars, there is nothing now but open fields of prairie grain. The old farm buildings are gone, buried in the past, but memories of that homestead live on in the hearts and minds of Grandfather's descendants. "Remember those who led you, who spoke the word of God to you; and considering the result of their conduct, imitate their faith" (Hebrews 13:7).

A Path for All Seasons

O Lord, how manifold are thy works! in wisdom hast thou made them all: the earth is full of thy riches (Psalm 104:24, KJV).

*A*t the back of our suburban home is a large wooded area that has become a sanctuary for local wildlife. Red squirrels chatter and scold one another like old maid aunts, and once in a while a Br'er Rabbit bounds forth from his brush pile to sample the delicacies of our vegetable patch. Even her highness the skunk occasionally deigns to stroll through these woods in solitary splendor, leaving behind only the lingering traces of her perfume, pungent on the cool morning air.

As the sun rises, the branches of poplars and scrub oaks seem to vie for space against the sky, sheltering the underbrush and offering welcome shade to timid violets. Enticed by the many dark secrets of the "forest," neighborhood children have forged a path deeper and deeper into these woods, and, following a winding trail, they eventually arrive at the very doorstep of the local school.

In September the goldenrod is in full bloom, and the leaves of the maple are tinged with scarlet. The hazelnuts are swelling within their fuzzy pods, and squirrels are busy from dawn to dusk filling up their pantry in

91

the hollow tree. Before long the burrs begin to cling, hitchhiking a ride on passing garments, traveling companions both bothersome and difficult to shake. Autumn smoke is in the air, and the children are pointing to the skies, trying to locate a passing flock of Canada geese.

The path is carpeted with fallen leaves now, yellow and rust and brown. Acorns in their miniature eggcups crackle underfoot, frightening away a rabbit whose coat is partly white and partly brown.

A family of bluejays display their brilliant plumage as they flit between white poplars. The skies are gray, and tomorrow a heavy snowfall will blanket the woods. Crimson clusters of shriveled highbush cranberries and red hawthorns will stand out against the newly fallen snow. Black-capped chickadees will appear as if by magic, as round and plump as little children bundled up against the cold.

For a time the woods stand braced against the winter, stiff and unyielding. Brilliant sunshine bounces off the path where thermal boots crunch diamonds underfoot.

At last a south wind blows, softening the shadows of the tree trunks, and branches begin to flex and bend in rhythm with the spring. Short clumps of pussy willows wait in hiding and overhead a pair of jet black crows circle and perch atop a bare but sturdy oak.

Spring rains fall gently, polishing the glossy red willows and swelling the buds to bursting point. Soon the air is heavy with the perfume of chokecherry blossoms. The emerald leaves of young poplars tremble and flutter in the breeze, a camouflage for robins' nests.

The days are hot and humid now. Moss grows thick and green on the shady side of tree trunks, padding the crevices, covering the foot of the ash tree with a velvet robe edged in toadstools. Fat bumblebees hover over the last of the wild roses, and clouds of mosquitoes swarm up gray along the path. For a time the woods will be deserted, as nature in peaceful dignity replenishes herself.

When the school bell rings in fall, however, delighted children will once more hop and skip along a path for all seasons, their lives, and mine, enriched by the wealth of God's creation.

Bridging the Years

Then the Almighty will be your gold
And choice silver to you (Job 22:25).

I can remember driving down an old country lane when the handsome young man beside me made a rather startling statement.

"I dare you to put your arms around my neck and give me a kiss," he said. Just like that.

Being young and impetuous, I accepted the challenge, for I was, after all, very fond of him.

The spot where we exchanged that first kiss is marked by a narrow bridge, and we have driven that road a hundred times in the intervening years, but somehow he always maneuvers things just right, and I always get my kiss.

As we cross that bridge my heart skips back about twenty-five years, and I realize this is the spot where two lives merged, where two winding trails became one path, and we sealed the place where they crossed with a kiss.

We have since looked back in dismay at the spontaneity of young love, realizing again and again that marriage has had such long-range consequences.

I think back to the hours of soul-searching prior to our wedding, when we wondered aloud whether other young couples were plagued by similar feelings of uncertainty. We sensed strongly the limitations of our own strength, and promising to "love one another until death do us part" was such a solemn vow to make. What if that love didn't last?

It was as if the perceptive young man who performed the ceremony knew our thoughts, for he chose Luke 24:15 as our wedding text: "Jesus Himself drew near, and went with them" (KJV). The Emmaus road stretched out beyond, and we crossed the bridge of matrimony with renewed confidence, for God Himself would go beside us.

A year later in a hospital room crowded with emergency equipment I gave birth to a tiny premature son, and we had crossed the bridge into parenthood almost before we knew it. Perhaps it is just as well, for if we had ever surmised the adjustments that are involved with a first child, we might have reconsidered! He thrived despite our awkward failures, and the experience was sufficiently satisfying to warrant three more

trips down the same road and over that same bridge into parenthood. Each time the way seemed just a little more familiar, just a little more delightful, perhaps because there were more of us to share in the adventure.

There were times, however, when we arrived at a crossroads and had to deliberate hard and long before reaching a decision. Would we take the advice of well-meaning friends or follow our own intuition? Would God have us risk the little-known trail with all its ups and downs, or should we stick to the well-traveled highway?

Such was the decision that faced us when my husband's health indicated that he should give up the teaching profession for a less strenuous job. It meant abandoning the familiar road that was dear to his heart and forging a path into the unknown world of computers. I watched apprehensively as he in faith made the sharp descent from the classroom, crossed the bridge of economic hardship, and began the slow but steady climb toward a new field of endeavor.

Not many years later we were confronted with the possibility of owning our own home, providing we build it ourselves. Swinging from scaffolds, feeding the baby, lugging shingles up a ladder, fixing the lunch, measuring twice and sawing once—it was not the conventional approach to independence. But when the sawdust had settled, we stood back with our arms around each other and realized we had not only built a house, we had also established a home, for every nail represented the cooperative effort of the whole family. We had crossed the bridge that leads to mutual appreciation.

There are other bridges I have not mentioned—the bridge of opportunity, which led us to a new community and another fellowship, and the bridge of enrichment, which opened up a whole new world of friends. There was the bridge of convalescence, which took us from sickness back to health, and the bridge of separation over which a loved one crossed, and we were left behind.

I expect that in the not too distant future other bridges will loom up ahead, and one or two may even take us by surprise while we are busy "communing together and reasoning," as married couples do. Looking back, however, we will realize that every major change was but a milestone and every new beginning a bridge on the Emmaus road of matrimony, a point where Jesus Himself draws near and goes with us.